Read All About
DOGS

by Jaclyn Jaycox

raintree
a Capstone company — publishers for children

Raintree is an imprint of Capstone Global Library Limited, a company incorporated in England and Wales having its registered office at 264 Banbury Road, Oxford, OX2 7DY – Registered company number: 6695582

www.raintree.co.uk
myorders@raintree.co.uk

Designed by Kayla Rossow
Picture research by Morgan Walters
Production by Katy LaVigne
Originated by Capstone Global Library Ltd
Printed and bound in India

978 1 3982 0320 4 (hardback)
978 1 3982 0319 8 (paperback)

British Library Cataloguing in Publication Data
A full catalogue record for this book is available from the British Library.

Acknowledgements
We would like to thank the following for permission to reproduce photographs: Capstone Studio: Karon Dubke, middle left 21, 28, right 30, bottom left 31; Shutterstock: Africa Studio, middle 14, bottom 18, middle 22, Aggata, top right 18, angelbandala, (top right) Cover, Cheryl Casey, bottom 23, ChiccoDodiFC, middle right 7, cynoclub, bottom middle 11, ded pixto, middle left 13, El Nariz, top right 14, Eric Isselee, 8, top right 9, middle left 9, bottom middle 9, bottom right 9, top left 10, top middle 10, bottom 15, Erik Lam, top right 10, ESB Professional, 24, Everett - Art, top left 6, bottom right 6, Grigorita Ko, bottom 13, Grisha Bruev, top right 11, Holger Kirk, bottom 29, Ivanenko.PRO, 1, Jagodka, middle right 17, Jamie Hall, top right 22, Jemastock, design element, Jim Cumming, 4, Kandapa, top left 26, Kelvin Degree, design element, Khanittha Anantasakdi, top left 27, l i g h t p o e t, bottom 14, L.F, 16, Lenny278, bottom right 21, Liliya Kulianionak, top , Litvalifa, tope left 19, Marcin's Prospect, bottom left 17, Michael Pettigrew, 12, Mostovyi Sergii Igorevich, 20, MykolaMoriev, middle left 10, Nagel Photography, bottom left 25, Noppanun K, (watercolour) Cover, oksana2010, middle right 25, Olimpik, top left 31, otsphoto, top right 13, Paya Mona, top right 15, ReVelStockArt, design elements, Rob van Esch, top left 29, Shaun Barr, bottom 7, Summer Hoover, bottom right 19, Svetlana Valoueva, top left 25, Switlana Symonenko, middle right 29, Tara burnsss, top right 21, Tatiana Katsai, bottom right 10, ThamKC, bottom right 27, thka, (bottom) Cover, Tikhomirov Sergey, top left 17, Vitaly Titov, middle right 31, Volonoff, design element throughout, WilleeCole Photography, top right 23, bottom right 26, Yuriy Chertok, bottom 5, Zivica Kerkez, middle left 30

Every effort has been made to contact copyright holders of material reproduced in this book. Any omissions will be rectified in subsequent printings if notice is given to the publisher.

All the internet addresses (URLs) given in this book were valid at the time of going to press. However, due to the dynamic nature of the internet, some addresses may have changed, or sites may have changed or ceased to exist since publication. While the author and publisher regret any inconvenience this may cause readers, no responsibility for any such changes can be accepted by either the author or the publisher.

Contents

Words in **bold** are in the glossary.

Chapter 1

History of dogs

Did you know there are about 900 million
dogs in the world? Dogs are popular pets.
But where did these furry friends come from?

Scientists think dogs came from wolves.

fox

Foxes, coyotes and jackals are all part of the dog family.

All dogs belong to the same **species**, called *Canis lupus familiaris*.

Dogs are **mammals**. Mammals breathe air and give birth to live young.

5

Humans have been keeping dogs as pets for thousands of years.

Some of the first dogs were used for hunting and guarding houses.

Dogs have even fought in wars as soldier dogs.

Some dogs work with police officers. Others help farmers to herd sheep.

Chapter 2

Dog breeds

There are many **breeds** of dogs. Each one looks and acts a bit differently. Every breed has something special about it.

There are more than 300 breeds of dogs!

Dog breeds are split into seven groups: sporting, hound, herding, working, terrier, toy and non-sporting.

Purebred dogs have parents that are the same breed.

"Designer" dogs have parents that are two different breeds.

Labrador retrievers are the most popular dog breed.

Spaniels have lots of energy and like to hunt.

English bulldogs can be couch potatoes!

Basenjis are one of the oldest dog breeds. They lived in Africa around 6000 BC.

Mastiffs are the heaviest breed. They can weigh 91 kilograms (200 pounds).

Chihuahuas are the smallest breed. They are shorter than a pencil!

11

Chapter 3

Life cycle

Dogs go through life cycles, just like people. They start as playful puppies. It's not long before they become fully grown adults.

Dogs go through four stages of life: puppy, adolescent, adult and senior.

Females give birth to a group of puppies called a litter.

Puppies can't see or hear for the first couple of weeks of life.

Puppies grow fast! They gain half their body weight in the first few months.

13

A dog's first year is equivalent to 15 human years!

Dogs reach their full size between 1 and 2 years old.

A dog learns to understand about 165 words in its lifetime.

By 2 years old, dogs have reached adulthood.

On average, dogs live for 10 to 14 years.

Small breeds usually live longer than large breeds.

Chapter 4

Dog bodies

Dogs can be different sizes and colours. But a lot of our four-legged friends' bodies are alike. And some body parts have special uses.

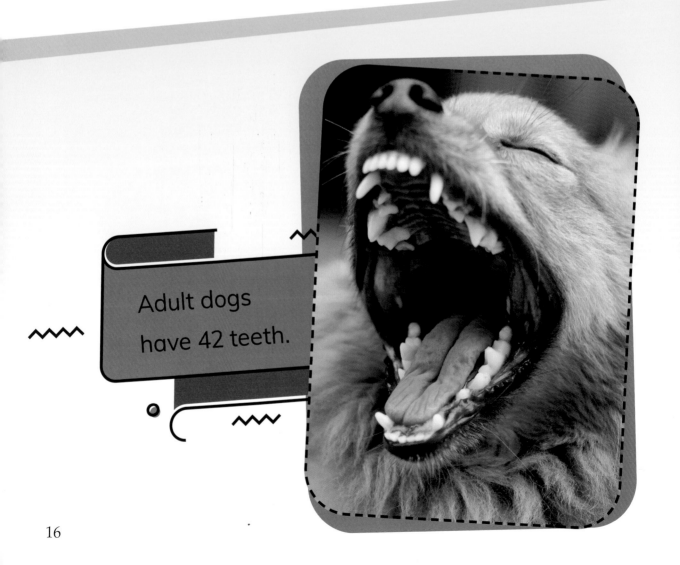

Adult dogs have 42 teeth.

A tail helps a dog to swim. It also helps a dog keep its balance.

Ears that stand up are called pricked ears.

Every dog has a different nose print.

Most dogs have brown eyes.

A dog's hind legs are bigger and stronger than its front legs. But a dog carries most of its weight on its front legs.

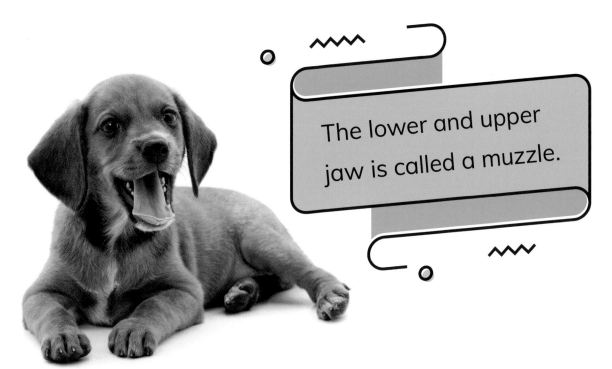

The lower and upper jaw is called a muzzle.

Whiskers help a dog "see" by feeling things around its nose.

A dog's fur keeps it warm. A dog can shed fur in the summer to stay cool.

Chapter 5

Senses

Dogs have amazing **senses**. They can hear and smell things that we can't. Let's take a look at the world through a dog's senses.

Dogs can see some colours. They don't see shades of red.

A dog's sense of smell is 10,000 times better than a human's!

Dogs can hear sounds too high or low for humans to hear.

Puppies can sense heat with their noses. It helps them to find their mothers when they can't see.

Dogs can see best at dawn and dusk.

We might catch the scent of a biscuit. But a dog can smell every ingredient!

Dogs don't have a strong sense of taste. Humans have five times more taste buds than dogs.

Dogs can use smell to know how someone feels. They know if their owners are happy, sad or scared.

Chapter 6

Dog behaviour

From chasing tails to slobbery kisses, dogs do some weird things. But why? Dogs can't speak. They "talk" using their actions!

Dogs lick people to show love.

Dogs will bark when they sense danger.

When a dog tilts its head, it is confused about something.

Dogs don't sweat. They pant to cool off. A dog breathes quickly and loudly when panting.

Tail wagging can mean a dog is happy or excited.

A tail tucked between the legs can mean a dog is scared.

Dogs may bite if they feel threatened.

Dogs wee on things to mark their **territory**. It tells other dogs what's theirs!

Dogs learn about things by smelling. That's why they sniff people and other dogs.

Chapter 7

Caring for your pet

Dogs make great family members. They are loyal, loving and protective. It's very important to take good care of them.

Make sure you keep your dog on a lead unless you are somewhere safe for him to run free!

Dogs need at least 30 minutes of exercise each day.

Dogs need fresh food and water every day. Maybe even some treats!

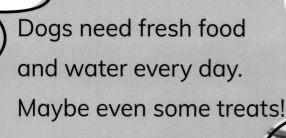

Dogs should have their own beds to rest in.

Dogs need a check-up with a **vet** at least once a year.

Injections called vaccines protect puppies from diseases.

Owners should brush a dog's teeth every day.

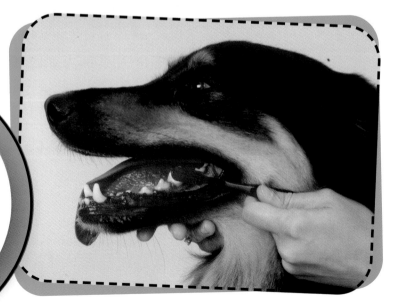

No one likes a stinky pup! Dogs should have a bath if they are dirty.

A dog should have a collar and ID tag in case it gets lost.

Dog training is important if you want a well-behaved dog.

Glossary

breed group of animals that look and act alike

mammal warm–blooded animal that breathes air, has hair and gives birth to live young

purebred having parents of the same breed

sense way of knowing about your surroundings; hearing, smell, touch, taste and sight are the five senses

species group of animals with similar features

territory area of land that an animal roams in

vet doctor trained to take care of animals

Index